The Wisdom of Rastafari

By

Rastafarian Group

Published by Left of Brain Books

Copyright © 2023 Left of Brain Books

ISBN 978-1-397-66773-1

First Edition

PUBLISHER'S PREFACE

About the Book

"This is a short anthology of quotes from Haile Selassie compiled by a Rastafarian group."

(Quote from sacred-texts.com)

CONTENTS

PUBLISHER'S PREFACE

PREFACE 1

ACKNOWLEDGEMENT 4

THE BIBLE 5

RELIGION 7

MORALITY... 8

HUMAN RIGHTS 10

UNITY.. 11

GOVERNMENT... 16

LEADERSHIP.. 21

EDUCATION 23

RESPONSIBILITY 27

PLANNING 29

WORK 30

SELF HELP 32

DEVELOPMENT.. 33

LAND POLICY 36

RESOURCES 38

AGRICULTURE.. 40

FINE ARTS 43

HEALTH... 44

INTER AFRICA 45

ETHIOPIA'S WORLD POSITION..................................... 46

INTERNATIONAL POLITICS 48

FATE.. 50

LIFE 51

DEATH 53

MISCELLANEOUS 54

PREFACE

IN that day shall this song be sung in the land of Judah; we have a strong city; salvation will Jah appoint for walls and bulwarks. Open ye the gates, that the righteous nation which keepeth the truth may enter in. Thou wilt keep him in perfect peace, whose mind is stayed on thee: because he trusteth in thee. Trust ye in the Lord God Jah Rastafari for ever: for the LORD JEHOVAH is everlasting strength.

For he bringeth down them that dwell on high; the lost city, he layeth it low: he layeth it low; even to the ground; he bringeth it even to the dust.

The foot shall tread it down, even the feet of the poor, and the steps of the needy. The way of the just is uprightness; thou most upright, dost weigh the path of the just. Yea, in the way of thy judgements, O Lord, have we waited for thee; the desire of our soul is thy name, and to the rememberance of thee.

With my soul have I desired thee in the night; yea with my spirit within me will I seek thee early; for when thy judgements are in the earth, the inhabitants of the world will learn righteousness.

LET FAVOUR BE SHOWN TO THE WICKED, YET WILL HE NOT LEARN RIGHTEOUSNESS; IN THE LAND OF UPRIGHTNESS WILL HE DEAL UNJUSTLY, AND WILL IDIOT BEHOLD THE MAJESTY OF THE LORD GOD JAH RASTAFARI.

selah, When thy hand is lifted up, they will not see, but they shall see, and be ashamed for their envy at the people, yea, the fire of thine enemies shall devour them.

Lord, thou wilt ordain peace for us; for thou also hast wrought all our works in us.

O Lord our God Jah Rastafari, other Lords besides thee have had dominion over us; but by thee only will we make mention of thy name. They are dead, they shall not live; they are deceased, they shall not rise; therefore hast thou visited and destroyed them, and made all their memory to perish.

Thou hast increased the nation, O Lord, thou hast increased the nation; thou art glorified; thou hast removed it far unto all the ends of the earth.

Jah, in trouble have they visited thee; they poured out a prayer when thy chastening was upon them. Like a woman with child, that draweth near the time of her delivery, is in pain, and crieth out in her pangs; so have we been in thy sight, O Lord.

WE HAVE BEEN WITH CHILD, WE HAVE BEEN IN PAIN, WE HAVE AS IT WERE BROUGHT FORTH WIND; we have not wrought any deliverance in the earth; neither have the inhabitants of the World fallen.

Thy dead men shall live, together with my dead body shall they arise; awake and sing, ye that dwell in dust: for thy dew is as the dew of herbs, and the earth shall cast out the dead.

Come, my people, enter thou into thy chambers and shut thy doors about thee; hide thyself as it were for a little moment, until the indignation be overpast. For, behold the Lord, God Jah Rastafari, cometh out of his place to punish the inhabitants of the earth for their iniquity; the earth also shall disclose her blood, and shall no more cover her slain. ISAIAH 26

ACKNOWLEDGEMENT

BLESSED is the name of the Lord God Jah Ras Tafari, and blessed is he who comes in the name of Jah, His Imperial Majesty Emperor Haile Selassie I and let the name of His glory be blessed.

So be it, so be it, so be it blessed.
This is the product of the combined effort of the Ras Tafari Brethren whose undying faith is in the Almighty, Everliving God, Jah Ras Tafari. He has given us the wisdom and understanding of His words that we might publish and manifest them among men.

Special mention goes to: Bro. Bob Blake, Bro. Clive Brooks, Sis Yvonne Brooks, Sis. Shirley Burke.
signed - United Africa

THE BIBLE

His Imperial Majesty
HAILE SELASSIE I
Emperor of Ethiopia, says:

WE IN ETHIOPIA HAVE ONE OF THE OLDEST VERSIONS OF THE BIBLE, but however old the version may be, in whatever language it might be written, the Word remains one and the same. It transcends all boundaries of empires and all conceptions of race. It is eternal.

No doubt you all remember reading in the Acts of the Apostles of how Philip baptised the Ethiopian official. He is the first Ethiopian on record to have followed Christ, and from that day onwards the Word of God has continued to grow in the hearts of Ethiopians. And I might say for myself that from early childhood I was taught to appreciate the Bible and my love for it increases with the passage of time. All through my troubles I have found it a cause of infinite comfort.

"Come unto Me, all ye that labour and are heavy laden, and I will give you rest" who can resist an invitation so full of compassion?

Because of this personal experience in the goodness of the Bible, I was resolved that all my country men should also share its great blessing and that by reading the Bible they should find truth for themselves. Therefore, I caused a new translation to be made from our ancient language into the language which the old and the young understood and spoke.

Today man sees all his hopes and aspirations crumbling before him. He is perplexed and knows not whither he is drifting. But he must realise that the Bible is his refuge, and the rallying point for all humanity. In it man will find the solution of his present difficulties and guidance for his future action, and unless he accepts with clear conscience the Bible and its great Message, he cannot hope for salvation. For my part I glory in the Bible.

RELIGION

WE are gratified in particular, to note that the work of this conference has been concerned purely with religious, spiritual matters free from extraneous political considerations.

This is only fitting and proper, for the church, as a symbol of peace, must follow the path of peace in all parts of the world. For world peace can only be made abiding by the grace of God, through the prayers of the Holy Fathers. The truth of this cardinal fact is evident to all mankind.

Therefore, it has become the noble responsibility of Christians, and peoples of other faiths and their leaders throughout the world, to pray and to work hard for the preservation of world peace.

We have always been religious, ever since childhood, ever since the day our father, Ras Makonnen, taught us the commandment of Our Lord the Creator.

But we don't consider our religion alone valid and have granted the people the freedom to observe any religion they please.

We believe in the reunification of the churches, which is why we were so happy to meet Pope Paul VI during our voyage to Italy. We were greatly taken with him, we judged him a man of superior capacity, especially as regards his intention to work towards church unity. He received us with great friendliness.

MORALITY

ITS BETTER TO GIVE

WISE men have always known the deep and pervading truth that it is better to give than to receive, for even as it conflicts with selfish and ambitious desires, it moderates and controls them.

Giving always demands sacrifice. To overcome the temptation to enjoy mere daily comfort, to press resolutely and patiently forward on the scheduled way, are true tests of the high degree of determination that should bind you together. Memories of past injustices should not divert us from the more pressing business at hand.

We must live in peace with our former colonizers, shunning recrimination and bitterness and fore-swearing the luxury of vengeance and retaliation, lest the acid of hatred erode our souls and poison our hearts.

Let us act as befits the dignity which we claim for ourselves as Africans, proud of our own special qualities, distinctions, and abilities. We must speak out on major issues, courageously, openly and honestly, and in blunt terms of right and wrong.

If we yield to blandishments or threats, if we compromise when no honourable compromise is possible, our influence will be sadly diminished and our prestige woefully prejudiced and weakened.

On this day which men of earth and angels of heaven could neither have foreseen nor known, I give thanks unutterable by the mouth of man to the living God who has enabled me to be present among you.

Today is the beginning of a new era in the history of Ethiopia.

Since this is so, do not reward evil for evil, do not commit any act of cruelty like those which the enemy committed against us. Do not allow the enemy any occasion to foul the good name of Ethiopia.

We shall take his weapons and make him return by the way he came.

We believe in cooperation and collaboration to promote the cause of international security, the equality of man and the welfare of mankind.

We believe in the peaceful settlement of all disputes without resorting to force. And in accordance with the charter of O.A.U. we will strive to eradicate colonialism, racism and apartheid from the face of the earth, to frustrate the efforts being made by foreign powers to dictate the destiny of the African continent, and we will continue to stand.

HUMAN RIGHTS

COLONIALISM and the policy of racism impose soul searching questions of human rights, weighing equally on the conscience of all men and nations of good-will. History amply shows that the freedom enjoyed by the many becomes fragile when the denial, even to the few, of basic human rights is tolerated.

Our efforts as free men must be to establish new relationships, devoid of any resentment and hostility, restored to our belief and faith in ourselves as individuals, dealing on a basis of equality with other equally free people.

We believe in cooperation and collaboration to promote the cause of international security, the equality of man and the welfare of mankind.

We believe in the peaceful settlement of all disputes without resorting to force.

All well ordered and modern states can only base themselves upon Courts of Justice and Conduct of Laws which are just, correct and geared towards the protection of the rights of individuals. Justice is a product of education.

Man's ingratitude to man is often manifested in willingness to relegate human beings to the scrapheaps of life when they enter the twilight of their careers and younger brains and stronger arms are found to replace them.

UNITY

ETHIOPIA is a nation fully committed to African unity and to the greater guise of world peace and shall continue to support and strengthen the O.A.U., which was established as an African instrument for peace and progress.

O.A.U.

The Organization of African Unity, is an organization which the people of our vast continent have established with a view to performing certain specific tasks.

Briefly speaking, the organization is established for the purpose of protecting in a better fashion, the independence of African States.

It is also meant to expedite the economic and social progress through cooperation of African peoples. It also has the important task of assisting in the maintenance of international peace and security.

We know that unity can be and has been attained among men of the most disparate origins, that difference of race, of religion, of culture, of tradition, are no insurmountable obstacles to the coming together of peoples.

We stand today on the stage of world affairs, before the audience of world opinion. We have come together to assert our role in the direction of world affairs and to discharge our duty to the great continent whose two hundred and fifty million people we lead. Africa is today at mid-course, in transition from the Africa of Yesterday to the Africa of Tomorrow. Even as west and here, we move from the past into the future The task on which we have embarked, the making of Africa, will not wait we must act, to shape and mould the future and leave our imprint on events as they pass into history.

We seek, at this meeting, to determine whither we are going and to chart the course of our destiny. It is no less important that we know whence we came. An awareness of our past is essential to the establishment our personality and our identity as Africans.

This world was not crested piecemeal. Africa was born no later and no earlier than any other geographical area on this globe. Africans, no more and no less than other men, possess all human attributes, talents and deficiencies, virtues and faults. Thousands of years ago, civilizations flourished in Africa which suffer not at all by comparison with those of other continents. In those centuries, Africans were politically free and economically independent. Their social patterns were their own and their cultures truly indigenous.

The obscurity which enshrouds the centuries which elapsed between those earliest days and the rediscovery of Africa is being gradually dispersed. What is certain is that during those long years Africans were born, lived and died. Men on other parts of this earth occupied themselves with their own concerns and, in their conceit, proclaimed that the world began and ended at their horizons. All unknown to them, Africa developed in its own pattern, growing in its own life and, in the Nineteenth Century, finally re-emerged into the world's consciousness. The events of the past hundred and fifty years require no extended recitation from us. The period of colonialism into which we were plunged culminated with our continent fettered and bound; with our once proud and free peoples reduced to humiliation and slavery; with Africans terrain cross-hatched and checker - boarded by artificial and arbitrary boundaries. Many of us, during those bitter yearn were overwhelmed in battle, and those who escaped conquest did so at the costs of desperate resistance and bloodshed. Others were sold into bondage as the price extracted by the colonialists for the 'protection' which they extended and the possessions of which they disposed. Africa was a physical resource to be exploited and Africans were chattels to be purchased bodily or, at best, peoples to be reduced to vasselage and lackey hood. Africa was the market for the produce of other nations and the source of the raw materials with which their factories were fed.

Today, Africa has emerged from this dark passage, Our Armageddon is past. Africa has been reborn as a free continent and Africans have been reborn as free men. The blood that was shed and the sufferings that were endured are today Africa's advocates for freedom and unity. Those men who refused to accept the judgement passed upon them by the colonisers, who held unswervingly through the darkest hours to a vision of an African emancipated from political, economic and spiritual domination, will be remembered and revered wherever Africans meet. Many of them never set foot on this continent. Others were born and died here. What we may utter today can add little to the heroic struggle of those who, by their example, have shown us how precious are freedom and human dignity and of how little value is life without them. Their deeds are written in history.

Africa's victory, although proclaimed, is not yet total, and areas of resistance still remain. Today, we name as our first great task the final liberating of those Africans still dominated by foreign exploitation and control. With the goal in sight and unqualified triumph within our grasp, let us not now falter or lag or relax. We must make one final supreme effort now, when the struggle grows weary, when so much has been lost, that the thrilling sense of achievement has brought us near satiation. Our liberty is meaningless unless all Africans are free. our brothers in the Rhodesias, in Mozambique, in Angola, in South Africa cry out in anguish for our support and assistance. We must urge on their behalf their peaceful accession to independence. We must align and identify ourselves with all aspects of their liberation and not fail to back our words with action. To them we say, your pleas shall not go unheeded. The resources of Africa and all freedom-loving nations are marshalled in your service. Be of good heart, for your deliverance is at hand.

1. One important lesson that we have learnt from the experience of the last ten years is that we cannot leave the further progress of African unity to take its own direction at its own pace without active guidance from us.

2. The volume of intra-African trade, which at present, accounts for less than ten percent of our total foreign trade should be progressively increased, so that by the end of the decade trade among African countries should occupy a significant place in the exports of each of our countries.

3. African countries should establish progressive targets for reducing tariffs and other trade barriers among themselves. Our Ministers charged with the responsibility of economic planning should hold regular consultations so as to harmonise our development policies and plans and to open up potentiala-venues for the expansion of intra-African trade.

Through regular consultations, we should undertake to identify the need for and to establish industries which may cater to our common needs.

This is important, because the scale on which modern industries can become viable today necessitates that we should create in Africa wide economic bases to support a balanced economic state.

GOVERNMENT

WHEN a whole nation accepts and maintains a government in existence, it means that the nation recognizes that government.

There is always something moving, brewing. There are ambitious people everywhere. Wicked people. The only thing to do is to deal with them with courage and decision. One must beware of uncertainty, weakness or conflicting emotions - they lead to defeat.

It is our opinion that the world has not changed at all. We believe that such changes have modified nothing. We don't even notice any difference between monarchies and republics: to us, they appear two substantially similar methods of governing a nation.

Democracy, Republic:
What do these words signify?
What have they changed in the world?
Have men become better, more loyal, kinder?
Are the people happier?
All goes on as before, as always.
Illusions, illusions.

One should consider the interests of a nation before subverting it with words. Democracy is necessary in some cases and we believe some African peoples might adopt it. But in other cases it is a handful, a mistake.

We are all adherent, whatever our internal political systems, of the principles of democratic action. Let us apply these to the unity we seek to create.

Force must be used against force. We ourselves, by virtue of our descent from the Queen of Sheba and King Solomon, ever since we accepted in trust, in 1916, first the regency of the Ethiopian realm and later, the Imperial Dignity, right up to the present, we have set out to the best of our ability, to improve, gradually, internal administration by introducing into the country western modes of civilization through which our people may attain a higher level.

In explanation of the notion 'gradually': unless it is through coaxing a child and getting it accustomed, it will not be pleased if one takes from it what it has seized with its hand. When one gives such a baby any sort of food, it will not wish to eat it, unless one shows it to the child and lets it taste it. Unless they give it milk or other soft food until it grows teeth, it will not be able to eat when they place bread or meat before them.

And similarly with people who have lived by custom only, without learning at school, without absorbing knowledge by the ear or observing and searching with the eye, it is necessary to accustom them, through educations to abandon habits by which they have for long been living, to make them accept new ways yet not by hasty or cruel methods but by patience and study gradually and over a prolonged period.

Only a system which tolerates dissent can survive

It gives us great pleasure to appear before this distinguished assemblage and we bring you the fraternal salutations of the Ethiopian people.

The people of Ethiopia and Trinidad and Tobago are joined in a massive and continuous effort to create for themselves a new and better way of life. They face many of the same problems.

The hopes and aspirations which they share derive from the same essential beliefs in the nature and destiny of man. It is thus inevitably true that there should exist between those two great peoples strong and lasting ties of friendship and understanding

Your role as the representatives of the people is a particularly critical one in the councils of the twentieth century. The manner in which a representative of the people should properly discharge his responsibilities has long been a matter for learned discussion among philosophers and political scientists.

The world of the developing nations is creating new problems for the scholars to ponder as new societies are emerging to deal with the intricate and explosive questions of national and institutional development.

Is a representative responsible only to a constituency or to the particular group or interest which has chosen or appointed him? Certainly this responsibility Must be an element in the thought and action of such a man, but there are higher values and greater interests and responsibilities than these.

Obstacles

Sectional, tribal and other divisive factors often pose major obstacles to national development. In their expanded sense, as narrowly national and ideological interests, they threaten unity and progress.

No one is today so foolish as to believe that any one nation constitutes a perfect monolith of faith and ideology. Nor could anyone wish that there should be such utter vanity of thought and aspiration.

The systems of Government which have sought to impose uniformity of belief have survived briefly and then expired, blinded and weakened by obsessive reliance upon their supposed infallibility. The only system of Government which can survive is one which is prepared to tolerate dissent and criticism and Which accepts these as useful and in any case, inevitable aspects of all social and political relations.

The tolerance of dissent and criticism within a Government proceeds from a single essential premise: that the Government exists to serve the people generally. Government servants, whether designated as representatives or not, have a trust to work for the general welfare.

The same trust exists among the member states of international organizations. The members of such organizations must adhere to some tacit or expressed conception of international welfare.

Common Goals

In the case of the Organization of African Unity, it is an African Unity, it is an African welfare; in the case of the United Nations Organization, it is world welfare.

In one way or another, the member nation must accept in thought, spirit and action the basic premise of their institutions that men of all races, beliefs and status share some essential-common goals.

From this premise, no great and easy actions follow as corollaries. The representatives of peoples and nations can only come together with open and objective minds and willing hearts to engage in dialogue, without rigid dogmas and slogans and without violence.

Working in this way achieves no instant Utopia. It may, however, enable us to achieve together what it is possible to achieve and to move forward steadily, if not always in great haste, with some degree of harmony and mutual understanding.

Domestically, we can build strong and happy and resourceful societies. Internationally, we can force the end of oppression of man by man and nation by nation. We can bring about the security and mutual trust which will open the way to the greater human achievements for which the needs of mankind now cry out.

(He concluded:) Permit me to express my heartfelt gratitude for the reception accorded me by the people and Government of Trinidad and Tobago.

LEADERSHIP

LEADERSHIP does not mean domination. The world is always well supplied with people who wish torule and dominate others.

The true leader is a different sort; he seeks effective activity which has a truly beneficient purpose. He inspires others to follow in his wake, and holding aloft the torch of wisdom, leads the way for society to realize its genuinely great aspirations.

The art of leadership is in the ability to make people want to work for you, while they are really under no obligation to do so. Leaders are people, who raise the standards by which they judge themselves and by which they are willing to be judged. The goal chosen, the objective selected, the requirements imposed, are not mainly for their followers alone. They develop with consumate energy and devotion, their own skill and knowledge in order to reach the standard they themselves have set.

This whole-hearted acceptance of the demands imposed by even higher standards is the basis of all human progress. A love of higher quality, we must remember, is essential in a leader. The true leader is one who realizes by faith that he is an instrument in the hands of God, and dedicates himself to be a guide and inspirer of the nobler sentiments and aspirations of the people.

He who would be a leader must pay the price in self-discipline and moral restraints. This details the correction and improvement of his personal character, the checking of passions and desires and an exemplary control of one's bodily needs and desires.

To be first in place, one must be first in merit as well.

He who has not learned to render prompt and willing service to others will find it difficult to win and keep the goodwill and cooperation of his subordinates. A leader will kindle interest, teach, aid, correct and inspire. Those whom he leads will cooperate with him in maintaining discipline for the good of the group. He will instruct his followed in the goals towards which to strive, and create in them a sense of mutual effort for attaining the goal.

EDUCATION

A strong nation and a free nation can only base itself upon education.

In order to make life worthwhile it is also necessary to acquire other things that can only come about after the acquisition of learning. Learning and technical training must be nurtured by faith in God, reverence for the human soul, and respect for the reasoning mind.

There is no safer anchorage for our learning, our lives and our actions than that provided by divine teachings coupled with the best in human understanding. The leaders developed here should be guided by the fundamental values and the moral power which have for centuries constituted the essence of our religious teachings.

These are crucial times when nations rise against nations, tensions increase and disaster is possible at any moment. Distances are shrinking. Peace and life itself are threatened by misunderstanding and conflict. Now is the time when man's relationship to God must be the foundation for all his efforts toward enlightenment, and learning the basis for understanding cooperation and peace.

The existence of a skilled and trained manpower is an absolute necessity for the progress and development of any country. Therefore, it is the sacred duty and responsibility of students and parents to see to it that the mistakes of the past are not repeated and that time which should be devoted to the pursuit of learning is not wasted by students heedlessly, following the instigation of a few misguided troublemakers who have yet to understand the value and the true meaning of education.

The salvation of our country Ethiopia, we have repeatedly stated to you, lies primarily in education. As Ethiopia is one, all Ethiopians are also one and education is the only way to maintain the condition.

In all countries of the modern world, special competence is required to deal with the advancement of agriculture, industry, commerce and the civil service. That competence, can be secured only through the facilities provided in modern universities.

We believe that the universities today stand as the most promising hope for constructive solutions to the problems that beset the modern world, problems which prevent the peaceful-cooperation of nations and which threaten the world and humanity with death and disaster.

From universities must come men, ideas, knowledge, experience, technical skills and the deep human understanding vital to fruitful relations among nations. Without these, world order for which we have so long strived, cannot be established.

A well informed public opinion is essential to the growth of political and social awareness. Only he who is informed can comment intelligently on his nation's development and only by such comments can errors be corrected and progress stimulated.

We must draw on what is valuable and meaningful in our history and tradition, merging this with the best in modern learning.

We expect from you, to whom we have given the opportunity of education in your chosen field great and productive service to our country.

If women develop in education, they can overcome the natural weakness and serve their country as men do.

It is our wish to assure the spread of education among all African People as much as among our own subjects.

A father should bequeath not only wealth but also provide proper education. Education has value when it is established in individuals of good character with respect to God. We wish that your destiny shall be embraced in an education firmly based in good character before men and respect before God.

Any who may wish to profit himself alone from the knowledge given him, rather than serve others through the knowledge he has gained from learning, is betraying knowledge and rendering it worthless.

A man's happiness is to make his brother happy, and to serve his country. Thus it is possible to justify for knowledge its high and deserved place. For knowledge is power. If it is not applied to its proper purpose, to create, let there be no doubt, it will destroy.

If we have made so many sacrifices for the education of our youth, it is because we are convinced that only through intellectual progress and education can Ethiopia come into its own and make it's just contribution to the history of the Middle East.

We believe that from truth alone is born liberty and only an educated people can consider itself as really free and master of its fate. It is only with an educated people that representative and democratic organs of government can exercise their influence for national progress.

RESPONSIBILITY

IT is both the duty and responsibility of the world's fortunate few to help fulfil the legitimate aspirations of the unfortunate many.

As man's faculty attains higher level of development and sophistication, so do his wants in life.

As generations come and go, those assuming responsibility for the period do not cease to try and improve on the past in order to meet newly arising demands. In this respect, it is quite evident that to march with the time members of the coming generation should build on what their forefathers have bequeathed to them.

It is because the present generation is cherishing and keeping intact what it has received from the past that it has succeeded in attaining its present stage of development, by making the necessary changes and improvements called for by conditions now existing. This would require great foresight and the-work accomplished as far as regards to this task of great responsibility is no small matter. It has been fulfilled as a result of God's blessing and His Divine guidance.

It is both the responsibility of the governor as well as elders to create harmony among the people in initiating them to discuss their common problems and work towards the problems and the betterment of their standard of living.

It is the duty of teachers to direct the thought and outlook as well as mould the character of their students. For this reason, the responsibility of teachers in training student - teachers aimed at the future progress and development of our country and the proper upbringing of students, could hardly be underestimated.

In the age in which we are living especially when different philosophies of life are competing against another, the responsibility of teachers has been even more exacting. Those who will be serving the people in future should follow this same path in endeavouring to develop their country and maintain her freedom. This is one of the main responsibilities of teachers.

In this age when man, through his knowledge of science, has created dangerous weapons to destroy himself the responsibility of the great powers for the maintenance of world peace is well known to everyone. We believe that the exchange of visits by statesmen to talk over matters on which their points of view will greatly help remove the misunderstandings and mistrust prevailing among States.

PLANNING

PLANNING is the basis of the rational and sustained use of capital, manpower and time in the acceleration of economic development.

The history of planning shows that no pioneer plans were ever executed even partially, much less wholly.

Planning is indispensable for the rational utilization of both a nation's resources and foreign aid or loans.

As a basis of, and working procedure for, a national socio-economic policy, a plan is a means whereby a nation can be developed through the rational utilization of manpower and machinery for the most important aspects of he country's needs.

The execution of any such plan needs, however, national participation. You must ensure that in your desire to achieve immediate goals, long term considerations of equal or greater importance are not ignored or irrevocably prejudiced. Plan your time and use both your physical and mental powers purposefully and productively. Military planning for the security of this continent must be undertaken in common within a collective framework.

WORK

EVERY labourer is a father, his labour is his child. Choose your project carefully and achieve it worthily.

Once a person has decided upon his life work and is assured that in doing the work for which he is best endowed and equipped, he is filling a vital need, what he then needs, is faith and integrity, compiled with courageous spirit so that no longer preferring himself to the fulfilment of his task, he may address himself to the problems he must solve in order to be effective.

Rich and poor have always existed and always will. Why? Because there are those that work and those that don't, those that wish to earn their living and those that prefer to do nothing. Those that work, that want to work, are not poor. For it is true that Our Lord the Creator sends us into the world as equals, but it is also true that when one is born one is neither-rich nor poor. One is naked. It is later on that one becomes rich or poor, according to one's desserts.

Yes, we too are aware that giving alms serves no useful purpose. For there is only one means to solve the poverty problem. Work.

We have said that whoever doesn't work because he doesn't want to is poor. We have said that wealth has to be gained through hard work. We have said those who don't work starve. And now we add that the capacity to earn depends on the individual: Each individual is responsible for his misfortunes, his fate. It is wrong to expect help to fall from above, as a gift:

Wealth has to be deserved. Work is one of the commandment of Our Lord the Creator!

If each and everyone endeavours to cooperate and work in as much as his capacity permits, our faith rests upon the Almighty God that he would bless the results for us.

It is not sufficient simply to see and admire the natural beauty and fertility of Ethiopia.

It is our obligation to work upon and benefit from this country whose fertile soil has been granted us by the Almighty God. We have to gain honour and pride for the country.

Whatever the task may be, man may begin it but he cannot complete it, unless God sustains and supports him. If he fails to accomplish the task on which he has set out, having worked to the best of his ability, he is not to be maligned by being called lazy.

SELF HELP

THE people themselves must come to realize their own difficulties in the development of their community and try to solve them by collective participation following an order of priority and taking their potentiality into account.

It is well known to you all that recognizing one's problems and striving hard to challenge them is a mark of an attempt at self-sufficiency. Self help in the benefits to be acquired through education, will save the individual from asking someone's assistance.

DEVELOPMENT

ALTHOUGH the beginnings of civilization of each country vary in time, the fundamental factors which gave impetus to each country to awaken and embark on the road to progress to reach their present level of development, are those qualities which are enshrined in the nature of man,namely desire and fortitude.

The partner who places his own short-range ambitions ahead of the long-range interests of the partnership has embarked on a course which will ultimately result in the dissolution of the partnership itself.

It is by the understanding of past difficulties that we can bequeath fundamental guidance which would be of pride to the coming generations we therefore urge our people to struggle and to make sacrifices for those things which will enable them to ameliorate their conditions of life and leave a richer heritage.

Economic Development

Where enterprise and initiative are not lacking, the pace at which the growth of a country's economy normally proceeds can be quickened or slackened by global developments far or near. In our effort to raise the living Standard of our beloved people, in our endeavour to bring prosperity to our country, the feeling of cooperation and understanding has always characterized our people.

A special case is the recent development in certain provinces where the people are seen voluntarily raising funds to build schools, clinics, roads and similar other projects. What can give one more pleasure than to see such a measure of self-help in one's life time, for the prosperity and progress of his own country? Let every citizen of our empire strive hard to strengthen this espirit de corps everywhere.

We entrust the spirit of good-will to our people to work diligently and cooperatively in order to arrive at the realization of this socioeconomic development that has been launched by either our government or our people. You have a rich land that yields a variety of products, do not be contented with the satisfaction of your bare needs but instead, cultivate your land among others with oleogenous plants, the seeds of which you can export for your greater benefit. Use the forest woods to make furniture and implements and exchange them for money. Your workmanship will be a monument to your name.

One should realize that thriftiness is the basis for the accumulation of wealth and the economic growth of a nation. One seldom minimizes the value of money earned by the sweat of the brow however small it may be, but for the extravagant even a huge amount of money is worthless.

The co-operative movement has long been known throughout the world, and we Ourself have on numerous occasions urged Our people to join increasingly in cooperative enterprises.

Co-operatives must, ultimately, play a highly important role in the growth of our economy, and no time can be lost in availing ourselves of the benefits to be derived from therm During the past year, we decided upon a programme designed to provide specific encouragement to the creation of agricultural co-operatives, and a number of Government-sponsored co-operatives, farms have been established by Our Ministry of National Community Development. We have provided lands, agricultural machinery and expert assistance to these farms and we entertain high hopes that their success will spur Our people to embark increasingly upon co-operative endeavours. Should Our people fail to avail themselves of this opportunity, the consequences will be regrettable indeed.

Community Development

The fundamental purpose of a community development movement is to teach the rural people of Our Empire that through cooperative self-help and a united approach to common problems, the vast potential for their own self-improvement which they themselves represent, can be translated into effective programmes which can do much to improve their standard of living.

Social Development

Lasting progress can only be built on deep and enduring foundations. When a solid foundation is laid, if the mason is able and his materials good, a strong house can be built.

To develop oneself, one has to develop one's own initiative and perseverance - a man has to strive in order to grow. Let us work out our own programmes in all fields - political, economic, social and military. Man's contributions which live to influence the life and progress of posterity, are the most permanent monuments that can ever be created. We must become increasingly willing to analyze our efforts, to experiment, to admit our failures as we take pride in our successes.

LAND POLICY

FOR those of you who possess the land and labour but lack capital, we have made credit available at low interest. For those of you who have the necessary finance but do not possess land to work on, we have, in accordance with our 'Proclamation' which entitles every Ethiopian to ownership of land, established offices in every province through which you may be able to acquire land. Those who have neither land nor money will be granted land and financial loan sat low interest. For those of you who possess land, who have financial resources and manpower, we have made experts available to furnish you with the necessary guidance and advice in your various undertakings.

Land Reform

The essence of land reform is, while fully respecting the principle of private ownership, the landless people must have the opportunity to possess their own land, that the position of tenant farmers must be improved, and that the system of taxation applying to land holdings must be the same for all.

It is our aim that every Ethiopian own his own land, in implementation of this principle. We have ourselves set the example by ordering that certain lands in Arussi Province heretofore administered by our Ministry of the Imperial Court be distributed to the tenants working on them, against payment by each man only of the nominal fees charged for the transfer and the registration of this property in his own name.

This has been the basic objective of virtually every modern programme of land reform; this is the ultimate goal of the study now being undertaken by the Committee of Land Reform.

RESOURCES

THE ultimate resource of a nation is its people. Unless this resource is employed for the benefit of the nation, unless the latent good which it represents is exploited to the maximum for the common good the nation will languish, poor in spirit, lacking in achievement.

But no people can make their full contribution to the life of the nation to which they over allegiance unless they possess and enjoy those few fundamental prerequisites indispensable to rendering their participation in the affairs of their country both possible and significant.

The growth of a people is complex and inter-related. Man must be educated; he cannot come to grips with or cope with or understand the modern world unless he has been taught about it. He must be assured of a minimum economic security; concern himself with matters going beyond the day-to-day satisfaction of his physical needs. unless he is fed and clothed and sheltered, nor can he acquire a sufficient degree of social consciousness to be able to support his own personal interests to the good of the nation and the development of its society.

Freedom, liberty, the rights of man, these mean little to the ignorant, the hungry, the ill-clothed, the badly housed.

It is our desire to see a much larger number of our young people benefitting from the resources we have our own and have received as aid from abroad, and our young people graduating in the fields of technology and industrial relation.

It is essential that, however great the sacrifice needed to curb economic stagnation maybe, available resources be as judiciously used as possible on a carefully selected list of priorities.

AGRICULTURE

SINCE Ethiopia's economy is predominantly agricultural, agriculture must play a large role in the plans which have been drawn up, at our command, for our empire's development.

It is the duty of all to apply the skill of their minds to the factories, the trading centres and the roads and communications which are also evidence of Ethiopia's prosperity, of Ethiopia's strength.

During the past year (1958) the abrupt cessation of rainfall during the growing season caused considerable damage to Ethiopia's crops. This experience has demonstrated that the rivers of our country should be devoted to irrigation, so that the food needs of our ever growing population will no longer be left at the mercy of the whims and caprices of the elements.

The fruits of the farmer's labour must be enjoyed by him whose toil has produced the crop. The uses of trees are many and varied. Groves of trees protect our fields and plantations from being desiccated by the desert winds which blow from neighbouring regions. During the summer months, they provide moisture and shade. If trees are not presently planted to replace those being cut down from time to time, our constant efforts to conserve and develop the wealth of our country through the welfare of present and future generations will be rendered ineffective and futile.

We are greatly grieved to observe the many thousands of gashas of rich forest land being destroyed every year by reckless timber-cutting, thoughtless forest burning, unregulated forest grazing and other misuses of our forest wealth, due to popular ignorance and desire for temporary advantage on the part of our people.

The existence or non-existence of forest wealth in a country is one of the most important factors influencing its development and progress. The increasing pace of deforestation and the growing dearth of timber in Ethiopia, caused by unregulated tree-cutting and the failure to replace these by new plantings, give us occasion for anxiety that a severe economic problem will confront the coming generation. It is essential that steps be taken here and now to stop this wastage and check this destruction.

In these days when all nations of the world, in recognition of the tremendous importance of forest wealth, have launched intensive programmes for forest conservation and re-forestation, it behoves our county also to take the appropriate measures to solve this problem.

It is our wish and our desire that each and every citizen of our country follow the example we set on this Arbour Day in planting this tree, and himself plant as many trees as he can, for his own benefit as well as for the benefit of future generations.

Without agricultural expansion, industrial growth is impossible. Great strides, it is true, have been made in introducing industries into Ethiopia in recent years. But in any less-developed agrarian country possessing only limited possibilities for selling the products of its factories in world export markets, industry can grow only if there exists an increasingly prosperous rural consumer population. Industrialisation is not an alternative to the development of agriculture; rather, the development of agriculture is the essential pre-condition to the growth of industry.

Measures will shortly be proposed to Parliament for action to be taken to preserve, for the benefit of present and future generations, the nation's forests which are not only valuable in themselves as a source of wood, but act as nature's guardian against the forces of erosion, which, unchecked, can transform fertile areas into barren and sterile desert.

FINE ARTS

A purely materialistic art would be like a tree which is expected to bear fruit without flowering and to sacrifice grace and beauty for mere utility.

Our admiration for the creator's handiwork should not be limited to those things he has provided us with for our daily needs, but should include all that is good and beautiful. It is these tender feelings of deep and silent admiration evoked from our hearts by the beauties of creation that should find adequate expression in the fine arts.

Music, drama and the other arts are rooted in the ancient history of our empire, and their development to an even higher peak of perfection will be possible in the atmosphere of a university. Ethiopia possesses an ancient literature and its study can be fostered here so that the Ethiopian youth inspired by this national example, may raise it to yet higher levels of excellence.

The study of the heroic history of our empire will stimulate the imagination of building authors and teachers.

HEALTH

THERE is nothing as precious to man as a sound mind in a sound body and it is essential that the physical well being of our people merits as much attention as its spiritual welfare.

INTER AFRICA

THERE is absolutely no doubt that Africans will eventually obtain their freedom and independence in spite of their present difficulties.

The people of African origin have emigrated to all parts of the world, but wherever they maybe, they have similar historical experience and the problems that await them depend on sympathy and this can be used by all of us as the basis for the establishment of greater cooperation, which will be for our mutual benefit.

Haile Selassie to Parliament in Jamaica: The people of Jamaica, by and large, have originated in Africa. This gives us another basis upon which we can contract a healthy relation because of the fundamental similarity between us, that will in the long run contribute to a better maintenance of international peace and security.

The Organization of African Unity is an organization which the people of our vast continent have established with a view of performing certain specific tasks. Briefly speaking, the organization is established for the purpose of protecting in a better fashion, the independence of African States.

It is also meant to expedite the economic and social progress through cooperation of African peoples. It also has the important task of assisting in the maintenance of international peace and security. And in accordance with the Charter of O.A.U., we eradicate colonialism and apartheid.

ETHIOPIA'S WORLD POSITION

BECAUSE of her unity and independence, Ethiopia had and still has jealous enemies and aggressive dissidents.

It is therefore the primary duty of every Ethiopian to safeguard the unity and freedom that has been fortified since time immemorial by the courage and bravery of our forefathers. We have to maintain its integrity, to work and benefit from its existence.

Ethiopia is a nation fully committed to African unity and to the greater cause of world peace and subsequently shall continue to support and strengthen the O.A.U., which was established as an African instrument for peace and progress.

Ethiopia is, by her own choice, a nonaligned state. Our Policies on the vexatious international issues of the day have been declared to all, and our adherence to them is steadfast: the urgent imperative of universal disarmament, the settlement of disputes by peaceful negotiation, the supremacy of reason and logic over force and irrationality.

We insist that the way to peace among men and nations rests in the even-handed application and enforcement of the principles of the United Nations and Organization of African Unity: non-interference in the internal affairs of others, self determination for the remaining dependent peoples of the world, respect for the territorial integrity of independent states. In the conduct of the international affairs of our nation, we have placed high value upon personal contacts between peoples and leaders of nations.

Ethiopia is a peace-loving nation. Except for those times when it had to rise up in arms to fight-off aggression or to advance the cause of collective security; there is not one instance in history of Ethiopia provoking a conflict by violating territorial integrity or by interfering in the internal affairs of others, and there will never be any such instance. However, Ethiopia will never be found wanting in its efforts to strengthen its defence force, sustained as it is by the traditional valor of its gallant people, to thwart the designs of those who are bent on violating the freedom and unity of its people and its territorial integrity.

INTERNATIONAL POLITICS

IN matters of foreign policy we have been ever guided by three basic principles. First is our deep conviction that, where there is no lack of goodwill, all international disputes can be resolved through negotiations, without recourse to violence. An inevitable corollary of this belief is our firm conviction that all nations, whatever their political persuasions, can live together in peace.

Second is our unswerving devotion to the principle of collective security.

Third, flowing from the principle of collective security, is the necessity, in these anxious days when the major powers are engaged in a frantic arms race, for all countries which have accepted this principle and assumed a share of the responsibility for ensuring the peace of the world, to become ever stronger militarily.

As we have stated time and time again, we are firmly persuaded that the path to guaranteeing the peace of the world lies in supporting the principle of collective security and the United Nations Charter, combined with a progressive reduction of the armaments which are being built up throughout the world. The billions of dollars which are now wasted on this fruitless effort could with great benefit, be diverted into the constructive channels of aid for the economic growth of under-developed countries.

Personal Diplomacy

International friendship can be strenthened and deepened by the personal exchange of ideas between leaders of nations.

What the economically backward countries are looking forward to, however is the application of the money now dumped on destructive armament to the solution of economic problems.

The Need for Concerted Action

What is called for at this critical time is for the international community to move from mere rejection and condemnation to taking action. The international community has many options, but what has been lacking so far is political will.

The world is only now coming to realize what Ethiopia and Africa have long recognized, that peace, independence and prosperity of mankind can be achieved and assured only by the collective and united efforts of free men who are prepared to maintain eternal vigilance and about unceasingly to protect these most precious of God's gifts.

FATE

WHATEVER the task may be, man may begin it but he cannot complete it, unless God sustains and supports him. If he fails to accomplish the task on which he has set out, having worked to the best of his ability, he is not to be maligned by being called lazy.

Man may, at the onset, control the direction which events take, but once his choice is made, events soon escape his control and history proceeds by its own force and momentum.

LIFE

WHAT life has taught me on the question of racial discrimination, I like to share with those who want to learn.

That until the philosophy which holds one race superior and another inferior is finally and permanently discredited and abandoned. That until there are no longer first class and second class citizens of any nation; That until the colour of a man's skin is no more significance than the colour of his eyes: That until the basic human rights are equally guaranteed to all, without regard to race; That until that day, the dream of lasting peace and world citizenship and the rule of international morality will remain but a fleeting illusion to be pursued but never attained; And until the ignoble and unhappy regimes that hold our brothers in Angola, in Mozambique and in South Africa in sub-human bondage have been toppled and destroyed; Until bigotry and prejudice and malicious and inhuman self interest have been replaced by understanding and tolerance and good-will; Until all Africans stand and speak as free beings, equal in the eyes of the Almighty; Until that day, the African continent will not know peace. We Africans will fight, if necessary, and we know that we shall win, as we are confident in the victory of good over evil. It will be self deceiving and a waste of time to advocate dialogue with those who are not ready to listen, because it is obvious that the freedom of millions is not a commodity subject to bargaining.

It is a fact that young people have always been impatient. This international movement is therefore not surprising. Such movements sometimes bring useful ideas into the open, but very often these ideas turn out to be harmful and contrary to ordinary progress.

This impatience and agitation result in larue part from a misunderstanding of realities. We are convinced that young people must learn to use their heads rather than their fists. They should be heard, but also guided for the common good.

Young people will be young people. You cannot change the uncouth manners of the youth. Besides there is nothing new in that: there is never anything new under the sun. They can't know it because they lack experience, they lack wisdom. Examine the past: you'll see that the disobedience of the young has occurred all through history. The young don't know what they want.

Life is like the theatre - One mustn't try to understand it all at once and immediately. It is no longer amusing.

There are good men and wicked. The former should be made use of and the latter punished, without attempting to understand why the ones are good and the others wicked. We demand too much of men to be able to respect them...

That which man dreams of and to which he aspires, unless fulfilled in his own lifetime, can produce no actual satisfaction to him. It will be self deceiving and a waste of time to advocate dialogue with those who are not ready to listen, because it is obvious that the freedom of millions is not a commodity subject to bargaining. It is better to die free than to live as slaves.

DEATH

NOW, however, it has become your fate to obey the order of the great and merciful Lord, alot that befalls each and everyone of us in our turn.

As it were, after you had accomplished what was within your bounds, you have slept, but although you depart from us physically, you works and your name will always remain among us.

On the death of Prince Makonnen:

Mortality is man's inevitable course. We must patiently accept God's resolution in giving us Makonnen, the one whom he gave us to be the ornament of our life, and recalling him. Death changes everything, sweeps everything away. Even mistakes.

MISCELLANEOUS

THROUGHOUT history it has been the inaction of those who could have acted, the indifference of those who should have known better, the silence of the voice of justice when it mattered most, that has made it possible for evil to triumph.

The glorious pages of human history have been written only in those moments when men have been able to act in concert to prevent impending tragedies. By the actions you take you can also illuminate the pages of history.

When you make man rich in the honours of this world and appoint him above other creatures, that it be known that It is not for his merit but only through your benevolence and generosity.

Since no creature created in Your image and to Your pattern gives up hope that everything he begs of You will be done for him until the day You sever his soul from his body, we beseech You that Ethiopia should not remain with her freedom extinct and prostrate under an alien ruler, so that the mouth of her people be silenced for fear of a foreign governor, but rather, that You will save them by Your deeds of kindness lest they remain with their hearts oppressed through being deprived of their own Ethiopian ruler who was leading them towards civilization under a light yoke and with gladness

O Lord, abode of exiles, light of the blind, truth and justice are Your thrones. Receive us who have been exiled for our freedom's sake, who have had to leave our country on account of violent assault. In praying to You thus, it is not for our righteousness but for Your great mercies.

Technical and scientific advances have combined to raise mankind to a level of material achievement never before realized.

A house built on granite and strong foundations, not even the onslaught of pouring rain, gushing torrents and strong winds will be able to pull down. Some people have written the story of my life representing as truth what in fact derives from ignorance, error or envy; but they cannot shake the truth from its place, even if they attempt to make others believe it.

Sports being the symbol of fraternity and team work there can be no doubt of its utility or of the sound virtues which it develops.

Unemployment is harmful - it harms and damages the unemployed himself, his nation and his country. Employers should strive to create more jobs. Workers should attend to their work with diligence and vigour. These twin attributes are the cornerstones for progress.

I know of the love which the Jamaican people entertain for the people of Ethiopia and the welcome which you have given me this day is evidence of it. I know that the Jamaican people were very sympathetic when Ethiopia was occupied during the fascist regime. During that time, Jamaicans as well as others who had African blood supported the Ethiopian Liberation Movement. And now that we are free we must assume the responsibility to work for the greater unity of all peoples of African origin.

It is quite true that a country can achieve material progress alone. However, we know from the experiences of the past that international cooperation tends to quicken the pace for progress of individual countries.

This is again another area for us to think about and see in what way we can further expand the relations of the people of Jamaica and Ethiopia.

From another fundamental point of view, this is precisely why the O.A.U. has been established. It is because the African continent, which comprises more than 250 million people, if it were to remain divided among more than 30 states, their individual voices would not carry weight. It is precisely why, since there is an identity of interest, we have attempted to include Jamaica.

Also, so that we can carry this weight in the councils of nations, and also through the process of cooperation and expanded economic relations we might be in a position to quicken the pace of development of the individual member countries of the O.A.U.

www.ingramcontent.com/pod-product-compliance
Lightning Source LLC
Chambersburg PA
CBHW051249020426
42333CB00025B/3123